THE DANCING MAN

By the same author:

Poetry:

Hunger Games
Life Sentences
The June Fireworks
High Wire
Take Five (ed.)
Dark Cupboards New Rooms
This Cathedral Grief

Fiction:

The Blessing
A Winter Sowing

Narrative non-fiction:

The White: Last Days in the Antarctic Expeditions of Scott and Mawson 1911-1913

Literary and Cultural Criticism:

Dividing Lines: Poetry, Class and Ideology in the 1930s
Taking it Like a Man: Suffering, Sexuality and the War Poets
Kenneth Slessor

THE DANCING MAN

ADRIAN CAESAR

RECENT
WORK
PRESS

The Dancing Man
Recent Work Press
Canberra, Australia

Copyright © Adrian Caesar, 2024

ISBN: 9780645973242 (paperback)

A catalogue record for this
book is available from the
National Library of Australia

Cover design: Recent Work Press
Set by Recent Work Press

recentworkpress.com

ss

For my Families in England and Australia

and In Memory of

G. Caesar (1926-2018) and E.I. Caesar (1926-2020)

Contents

I

CLEARING THE HOUSE

II

SPACE WALKER VARIATIONS

III

VIEWS FROM THE MUNDANE

IV

THE DANCING MAN

I

CLEARING THE HOUSE

Coal-Fired

My family comes from mining country,
North West England, Mosely Common no. 1 pit,
where great-grandfather, great-uncles
hewed out a hard-earned crust from
narrow chambers underground.

I remember as a little boy
being scared of the coal-coated
men in their studded jerkins
who carried the nuggety sacks
with bent backs up the narrow path
to the coal-hole at our house
before the Clean Air Act came in.

And how I thought the old buildings
of Manchester, the chimneys, mills
and church spires, were hewn from
the same black stone not realising
they were soot stained brick.

It's easy to forget now coal
is just another dirty word,
how then black diamond meant
steam and power and light,
fuelled heat against the blistering cold,
made the dancing blaze of open fires
beguile a small child's staring
on frosty mornings, and through

the drear dark nights of winter
ignited seams of invention.
The flickering shifting devil shapes,
the scrolling smoke beckoned
towards this hazardous inheritance:
a creative mine of flame and dust.

.

Totem

I

Amid the merry junk and bric-a-brac
in the tourist village gift-shop,
a chart purports to show by birth date
my Native American totem creature.

I'm with my wife, daughter, grand-girls.
We're having fun. They are delighted
not vindictive, as they cry, You're a goose.
Silly needs no saying.

I join in laughter, see the round-hulled body,
the too short legs, long craning neck,
sharp featured beak, the ungainly waddle,
all my clumsiness.

But then I remember wild migrations
with sure compass and deliberation
in strict formation, the pink-footed geese,
every year their elegant resolve in flight.

II

A brutal time of loss
driving from the nursing home
in an English autumn of dark mourning
towards the old place I was clearing for sale
my father dead, my mother immobile
fogged in delusion, hallucination,
against a darkening sky, I saw

                                    grey geese

                       head of

       an arrow   full of   fast   purpose

                       in their

                                  certain flight.

Every year they land in fields that surround
the industrial decay of the suffering town
on their way to feed at Martin Mere
before their onward journey south
away from the vast freeze of Iceland.

                    I can't say how or why the sight
                    filled me with strange exultation
                    as if I soared with them carried by the
                    vast energy of their wingbeats.

migration

my own

It made   from home   to home

seem less

unnatural

Looking backwards there was also looking
forward, the possibility of charting a course
to let my task of grief become winged fuel
speeding me through the dark and lowering
passages towards a resting place
               in warmth and light.

III

In the abyss of days
following my father's death
sorting, packing, destroying
fifty years of family history,
on cool mornings I ran through the lanes
and fields beside the East Lancashire Road,
that depression gift to job-creation in the 1930s,
now a never quiet four lanes of heavy traffic
thundering between Liverpool and Manchester.
In this strange space, where agriculture abuts
the hectic scramble of desperate commerce,
the roar of bewildered decadence, the dying
whine of post-industrial decay, I heard
from behind a hedgerow a shrieking clatter.
I stopped to peer and saw a flock of pink-footed
geese resting and feeding in the field,
a sight of wonder, their honking psalm,
a comic hymn rising above the spew of diesel,
the tumbril din of vehicles,
this raucous goose choir provided
a magical balm, resounding
of all humanity has not yet destroyed,
the abiding promise of spirit's flight,

                              uncanny beatitude.

IV

Fourteen years old and the bombs falling—
my mother hiding beneath the stairs,
night after night with the world exploding,
her father's stories of the Somme, Passchendaele
translated now to the Manchester Blitz—
his weeping failure as an air-raid warden,
the lights and noise too much to bear,
too like the trenches—*We didn't go through
that to live it all again like this,* he said.

When I was small, my mother was
the teller of tales, singer of songs.
She would sit my sister and me on her knee,
arms around us and sing the old songs,
Irish and English folk tunes and nursery rhymes,
sly products of dark imagination:
the broken bough, the cradled baby fallen,
the house burnt down by the flaming tail
of an errant mouse, the leather-clad old
misty-moisty morning man, a sinister
wedding candidate. They stayed with me
through the years.

Now I seek to be the inheritor
of Mother Goose, spinner and weaver
of words, aspiring to intricate cloth,
no pantomime, following
my mother's skein, goose navigation,
the way their eyes detect magnetic fields, as
I explore co-ordinates of imagination,
light and dark, backwards and forwards,
to understand generations of fable—
the peerless ascent of arrowhead flight,
forging on through every catastrophe.

Heirloom

Why shouldn't I, he said, as he gave his watch to me,
as if asking himself an imponderable question,
voicing words of self-persuasion.

I think he knew he was dying
but wouldn't admit it or see a doctor
until it was too late for either of us.

I returned to Australia with the watch
I knew I'd never wear, but still
it was a token—the gift of time

measured in a gold case. The diagnosis
followed: three to six months they said.
Nothing to be done.

Stricken a fortnight later, he died
while I was on the plane.
Somehow it seemed a set-up—

he who never wanted me to leave
up and gone before I could get there
to say goodbye, leaving me

forever with those words
and his parting gift:
Why shouldn't I?

Scene from a Journey

At the coach station, waiting to leave Heathrow,
from a window seat I see a son parting from his father.
The older man is keen to embrace, he wants to cling.
The youth, eighteen or nineteen, can't wait to be away,
climbs aboard and takes a seat on the opposite side.

> He slumps and stares down
> into the road, his expression
> strained, his mouth a thin, grim line
> of anger or contempt.

On the kerbside his father dances in eagerness
to wave, to forge some last connection.
He capers and jumps beside the bus
to catch a glimpse. . .

> His son sees nothing of this,
> unmoved, unmoving
> staring at asphalt, longing,
> praying maybe, to be free.

How this drama haunts me and how
elusive what to wish for in the final scene.
Years later, will there be hugs of reconciliation,
maybe even the paternal kiss of blessing,

> or will it be the stiff, cold handshake
> that speaks of distance once achieved
> never to be crossed, pride unbending,
> the silence of differences never
> lost.

Stormy

It seemed too pat: after my father's death,
I noticed the clock in the breakfast room
had stopped. I was spooning my melancholy
cereal alone in the old place I had to pack-up
and sell. My parents lived in the house
for fifty years and for fifty years I never stopped
thinking it was somewhere I ought to be,
though for years on the other side of the world
I'd lived the paradox of home from home.

Now it was all about last times, my mother
removed to a nursing home, blind, her body wasting
mind deranged, moments of lucidity dwindling,
my days were about folding and throwing,
disposing their lives, trying not to let memories
turn to obsessive hauntings, my father's sepulchral
silences which I never learned to broach,
my mother's insatiable need to love and possess.

It was then I heard a loud crash as of something
or somebody tumbling in another room. Puzzled,
I hurried from kitchen into the empty hall where
on the floor fallen from the stairwell wall
the barometer lay broken, my father's retirement
gift smashed beyond repair, forever predicting storm.
It seemed his ghostly sleeve had caught it,
breaking a last silence as he rushed to leave
the violence of the promised weather, always falling.

Trig

It took too long for me to realise
the feelings you couldn't speak
were invested in things. So when
I was thirteen and you gave me
your antique geometry set,
protractors, dividers, square and compass,
symbols of true measure and containment
which, unselfconscious, I dismantled,
I didn't know I was hurting you so much.
I'm not sure Freud's oedipal trigonometry
explains our crossed lines. It was more
a matter of temperament. Bored to tears
with mathematics, I was longing to break
free, reading books beneath the desk,
while the endless ones and zeros of binary
numbers passed me by. Meanwhile,
the austerity of your silences, unspoken
emotion, the judgement of cold looks
remained manly signs I failed to intuit,
my passion beginning to seek the boundless
space of wild and loquacious art.
It was my mother who chastised my
destructive bent on your behalf,
spoke of how precious those instruments
were to you, how much they cost, implied
I was taking apart the love we shared
when I was a child. It was only years
after you died, I understood the sad fuel
that fired my mourning: a scalene triangle
of misunderstanding, love beyond reason
that has no measure, the unspoken
grief of broken circles.

Days of Coincidence

(For Richard and Andrew)

We came to Llanddwyn Island,
my brother and nephew, their partners and children,
a holiday on the first anniversary of my father's death,
the light bruised, weather uncertain.

The tide was out. We walked across the causeway
to the ruins of St Dwynwen's Church,
and read she was the Patron Saint of lovers,
her day, my day, 25ᵗʰ January.

A Celtic cross, another plaque
which tells of the old days when
shepherds lit candles here each April 25ᵗʰ,
St Mark's Day, to protect their flocks.

This weird coincidence of dates
my birthday, my father's birthday,
bound us again in unlikely pilgrimage:
the harsh cry of a seabird echoed my lamentation.

The clouds rolled in. It was so dark,
summer seemed defeated. The storm began.
We hurried back across broad sands,
the rain blown slant, stinging cheeks and legs.

It felt like chastisement
until I turned and saw my nephew
sheltering his son in his arms,
bearing his burden of love through the storm.

And I saw my teenage nieces
urging their toddler cousin on,

my brother hand-in-hand with his beloved
and knew my father's goodness in them.

To think of love warmed me then,
the creative spark, the sexual flame,
and the ancient candles of the flock-masters
lit to keep their lambs from harm.

Slow Fade

I try to hold my mother's hand as tears slowly leak
from rheumy eyes near sightless now, making
runnels down her ruined face. Her fingers, once so fine,
are bent and knotty like winter twigs they shake
and claw as if trembling in a fearsome breeze.
She hallucinates, sees fire and flood, smells burning,
there are flames at the foot of her bed,
water drips down the walls. She tells a friend
she's been to hell and back. If we must talk in metaphor
who could say she's wrong? A ghostly bride
dressed all in white descends from the apple tree
on an escalator. Small boys peep round corners,
little devils, making faces and rude gestures.
Itinerant butchers and fishmongers, tormenting,
leave their stinking wares to rot upon her blanket,
demand payment with menaces. I try to tell her
none of this is real. To no avail.
Feeding her, she asks, *What's that writing on your dress?*
I try to persuade her she's mistaken.
She says I am a liar. Who can say this isn't true?

There is no nobility here. Immobile, incontinent,
nearly blind and mostly deaf, if I say she's ninety-three,
I hear defensive voices protest: *What can you expect?*
You have to pay the ferryman.
But in what coin and for how long?
Is there any meaning to this suffering?
Life at any price, my mother seems to choose.
In a lucid moment says she isn't ready yet to leave us.
What transformation shall we invent to accommodate this pain?
Say, perhaps, that having had this glimpse of purgatory
we might be led to recognise with keener sense,

if we can ever find our way to it again,
the joys of life. Or is this a mere fantasia
scribed upon a frock to avoid acknowledging
a solemn truth: sometimes the kiss of death
is sweet and light, sometimes it is not.

The Use We Make of Them (Material)

I

There are days of safe research:
a life delivered in neat boxes,
library pleasures, the avid trawl
through wordy remains
of the famous, infamous life,
an eager rifling for evidence
digging for dirt, detective excitements,
to prove the exciting thesis
or justify the huge advance
on a doorstop biography,
the subject packaged to a paper brick;
no risk the live voice will object:
that isn't me, their mouth
stopped in cemetery soil or ash,
only print or holograph survives
from which to chisel
the neat or abrasive epitaph.

II

This is work of a different order.
Here is a terrible intimacy.
After my father's death, my mother
immobile, incontinent, lost
in memory and hallucination,
confined to a nursing home,
the archive in which I wander
is their house, the family home,
my task to be the arbiter

of fifty years' hoarding,
preparing the place for sale.
Risky undertakings in every room:
cupboards, bureau, wardrobes, drawers
stuffed with desolate remembrance,
accumulation of lives they couldn't afford
to discard, I become the reluctant
bin-bag boy, the life-disposal man
the cool destroyer with the black sacks
and shredder, junking cards, letters,
diaries, the commonplace cliches
with which they tried to fill
the desperate spaces of desire.

III

Day after day for months I discover
how the most ordinary objects:
watch, teacup, ornament, spoon
jacket, skirt, shoe and cap
conjure the wordless ghosts
the absent presence, the present absence,
avatars of love which leave me
at twilight in the gutted lounge
watching another sunset
through the picture window
the light old gold against the gloom
thinking about the paucity
of metaphor for tears,
while grasping my own trove:
look what I've mined already,
though I don't know yet what to make
from all this loss, all that's tossed,
or my mother's bewildered accusation:
I know exactly what you've taken.

Museum Pieces

(In the spare-room wardrobe)

I

At the back of a shelf, sealed in a plastic bag,
a jag of black metal with cutting edges,
small enough to hold in the palm of my hand.
On a torn scrap of paper, my mother's elegant script,
the notice of her material poem:
A piece of shrapnel which landed
on our dustbin lid during
the Manchester Blitz, December, 1941.
It recalls the stories she told, how at fourteen
she hurried through the blackout to meet
her mother from the mill before the planes
came over; of hiding beneath the stairs
while the bombs fell; and, how she walked
to the Christmas Panto that year
past smoking ruins of the broken city.
The relic holds the impulse to never forget
the unimaginable can happen:
steel can rain from the air hurtling
our capacity for the exact sciences
of violence. It is the souvenir which clatters
down the years, suggesting both the geology
and archaeology of anxiety and fear:
I find myself clutching a piece of bombshell
dropping the cold and jagged strata
of my unhappy inheritance.

II

Also stashed at the back,
an old cardboard box,
its green and blue floral pattern fading,
inside a black tin painting set,
another careful caption:
Given to me by Gladys Aldin,
a neighbour who was very kind to me,
in1937/8 when I was eleven or twelve.
I thought I was everybody—only
the well off kids had paint-boxes like this.

Twenty-four water colours, two thin brushes,
the small tablets of colour faded, dry and cracked,
concave with old use. For eighty years my mother
kept this reminder of childhood poverty,
a moment's elevation from *nobody* to *somebody,*
the cruel shades of class unconsciously preserved.
However far you thought you'd risen, here was
the evidence of where you came from. I wonder
if you ever saw the colours of art shine so brightly
or thought you were 'everybody' again.

III

The pathos of my sister's first shoe—
red leather, round toe, tiny strap and buckle
preserved in tissue paper. I recognise it
from studio photos my parents had taken
when she was two. Look, it seems to say, how far
we've come *No clogs, no barefoot urchin here.*
This is a souvenir of first faltering steps
into the middle-class, first celebration
of accomplishment, not knowing, maybe,
my sister's talents would outpace us all.
But why just one? Perhaps the pair would
remind too much of Goody Two Shoes,
rags to riches, or more likely signify
her growing up and walking away towards
an independence my mother never managed,
my sister fought all her life to achieve.
Now, too late, I place the shoe in the memory
box the kindly carer thought would help,
though my mother's body and mind are
lost to the sight or sound of any true
remembrance. Daily she asks where my
sister is, forgetting she has gone before,
dancing quietly out of our life too soon.
I remember her pink ballet shoes, their
silk ribbons, my mother didn't save.

IV

Strangely, they remind me of Miss Haversham's wedding table,
my mother's mementoes of her day of days, the plastic horseshoe,
the model bride and groom forever attached to a shard of icing,
fake as the hollow tiers of the austerity cake, rationing still the rule
in England after the war. I chastise myself. It's not as if these tokens
are reminders of jilted love; my parents' marriage lasted seventy years,
only in death did they part, yet these poor keepsakes somehow hold
the frail cobwebs of lost romance—marking the beginning
of a journey which ended in a cliché of tears. I recall
conversations in old age, my dad silent as my mum rehearsed
her needling griefs as if I might be the only one to stitch an answer,
though I had none. After an hour of complaint, she would sigh
and say, 'of course I know how lucky I've been, how lucky I am.'
Later, they had cross words, rows, recriminations as my father
tried to nurse her through immobility, delusions, incontinence
of mind and body. He died first. Now they have both gone into
the dark two years apart, leaving this horseshoe and the miniature lovers,
the icing on the cake, I don't know what to do with.

V

Instead of shoes, beneath the vacancy
left by empty hanging space,
a raucous discovery of sorrow
stacked in neat rows a library of
Aussie Women's Weekly diaries
we posted every year because you said
they closed the miles between us.
I didn't know you wrote an entry every day,
your scholarship from back streets to
grammar school shining through
that elegant hand, though not a word
was *literary* in the record of your days,
their quotidian pleasures, meals cooked,
friends invited, the garden harvest,
meetings of your philanthropic clubs.
An irony I only heard an hour of misery
via telephone every week,
the complaints of age to which I had no answer.
When I found the diaries, and knew there were
too many to save or transport
you were in the nursing home lost in time
and delusion; I had to chuck your past
yet chose a few years to keep.
They're in my wardrobe now.
I won't read them for some time
not wanting to indulge.
Still, I remember my favourite entry
cast against the gloom you shared
with me. In May or June,
the English spring, in old age,
you wrote with no hint of disaffection
or dismay: *Another beautiful day.*

VI

There are remains beyond conservation.
Your Irish family used to send presents
for Christmas: embroidered handkerchiefs,
Belfast linen with hand-stitched blooms,
petals that might bleach but never fall,
I found some yellowing in a drawer.
The pressed-flower pictures you made
look like them: all too pretty, too decorative
for art, truly life stilled, somehow achieving
the opposite of their intention to preserve.
I wonder if that's why you stopped making them
and couldn't bear to cast away the remains—
another strange trove I discovered
on an obscure shelf, pressed
between pages of an old encyclopaedia
on sheets of blotting paper,
poignant footnotes to the idea of knowledge,
fragile remnants of primrose, daisy, forget-me-not—
they crumbled to pastel dust as I binned them.
In the paling of those vibrant colours
I recognised their poem: the defeat
of your aspiration, though those faded pictures
were left on the wall for me to give away
or throw, while outside the garden bloomed

$\qquad\qquad\qquad\qquad\qquad\qquad$ and died.

VII

Emptied, there only remains
the top of one wardrobe to be cleared,
the row of teddy bears my mother sewed,
propped against the wall,
behind the plastic warship my father made
after he retired. These look like evidence
of second childhood. But I don't know.
My parents' early lessons included
those from aerial bombardment:
how easily lives, houses, and all within
could be blown away. What meaning
might survive such rendering to dust,
how much might need to be preserved
to store up a belief in tranquility?
Soft toys and battle cruisers sit like guardians
of the other treasures that filled each space
for solace and protection.
When I've cleared them all away,
only these words will be left to curate
exhibits consigned to memory,
as if they might survive a firestorm
to comfort and defend.

The Three of Us

I

My sister was autumn's daughter.
How she loved those burnished colours
russet, pale gold, deep green to match
her Irish eyes. She was fond of quoting
Keats, season of mists and mellow
fruitfulness etc. An irony she didn't
ripen to old age, scythed before her time,
she didn't live to sing the funeral songs
of spring for our parents. We buried her in
summer woodlands before the first leaf fall.

II

I am the child of winter,
the northern January boy.
My early days were dark days
lit only by frost and snow,
colour blind, the stark intricacy
of leafless branches,
charcoal tracery against
grey skies became me.
I gave my mother grief
in leaving—an attempt
to thaw myself under
the Australian sun, the
massive skies and horizons
an escape from the huddled hearth,
cracked patterns of frost
on the inside of the window
panes, only to find, as if
I couldn't escape my destiny,
on the Tablelands of New England
and in Canberra, the perishing
winter mornings, ice on the paddocks,
the cold, my cold, inescapable.
I shivered as I watched my mother die
in the English spring.

III

As my mother lay dying, my brother
brought her jonquils, small daffodils
she always used to say reminded her
of the day she birthed him. *It was a time*
of such great joy, my parents said,
the arrival of this last, late-born child.
Austerity was over, they had climbed
into prosperity. It was spring.

His tribute of flowers made me feel
I had nothing to give. We arranged them
on her windowsill. I like to think they were
the last splash of colour her near sightless
eyes discerned. They were still there,
shining gold, the day she died.

The Last Crop

With September came the ripening
of the apples. The old, gnarled tree
I'd known since childhood was covered
in green bounty I had no use for.
In past years my parents would have
picked the Bramleys, peeling, coring,
slicing for apple sauce, pies and crumble,
stored in the freezer for feasts year-round.
Now, it was all over, the house up for sale
and I living there alone with the ghosts,
daily sweeping and lifting the windfalls
until bucket loads became sackfuls
some of them smashed, invaded by wasps,
rotting beyond repair. Allergic, I wore
my father's ancient gardening gloves
as I cursed the bumper crop, resenting
the way the bins hummed and buzzed,
dangerous with cider-drunk, drowsy insects,
while I inhaled the sweet smell of decay,
the broken flesh of fruit alive with stings.

Helpless

There are no streetlights in this bleak metropolis,
a concrete nightmare of stark planes and spaces
no traffic bothers overpass and beckoning tunnel.
Sky scrapers obscure as ancient monoliths rear
above rain-slick roads, empty pavements,
the only illumination arc lights over the
abandoned bus-station, its empty shelters,
where we stand, my companions and I,
lost and wondering what to do. They are dead.
We are desperate to find our way to my sister,
who has gone before. I hail a cab, it slows,
the hunched and hooded driver peers at us,
then drives past into the gloom. I promise
my mother and father I will help them, though
it's too late for transport. The rain keeps falling
as fast cars drive away in silvered splashes
and I stand waving to the vacant streets until I wake,
alone, lying in the dark, with no ride to take.

II
SPACE
WALKER
VARIATIONS

Space Walker Anticipates

The ultimate step

                                            outside

to be some time   free-

                  floating

nowhere   staring at   somewhere

                  weightless

nothing to heft   breathing pure   artificial   air

sans everything but   a view of   our pallid star

                earth as
      whey-faced lune   preposterous distant home
   all its features blanked   to a blue and silver dish
 a patterned splash of glory   on a black gallery wall
        a brilliant   light-filled abstract
       the human erased

but for my goggling   eye exploring   this broken

     unbroken

                    loneliness

hoping   it might lead to   a sense of comic

cosmic acceptance   the astronaut as clown   saluting earthly love amidst a glitter   of star ice   sending

     scattered   signals   back

    there is no gravity here

I can't stop   *smiling*   *watch this*

    space.

Space Walker's Abstraction

          Staring back

to earth

          the perspective

is all pattern

          a wash of creamy

cloud and ocean

          a plate of Stilton soup

good enough

          to eat.

How everything

          turns back

to hunger.

          Is it escape

or encounter

          this exploration

without utility

          as outer space

becomes inner

          a process between me

and the world

          made abstract

in which it's

          possible to love

the idea of people

          to remember acts of kindness

to long for arms

          that hold and fire

without lead or boredom

bullets or plain old hatred
the gun-toting
madman in the
gore-soaked mall?

There's a lot to be said
for distance
making fonder the thumping
muscle in the chest
small blessings and mercy:
there is no news here.

Space Walker at Play

Free

                                      floating

        cutting ties

that bind   saying   goodbye to

                         gardens wild with blossom

training   for loss

doodling   this space

        treading   weightless

light   in the dark

                                     clarifies the view—

no need for media pundits
the busy distraction
of multiple screens
pods, phones, ibook etc
the useless cackle
of political games

                                           jump

here   you can

                             and tumble

      like a

                  manic gymnast

        thrill-seeking

                                        while the globe

transformed to an   aesthetic

                                        whole

suggests something   might be   gained   from

          renunciation

     this willed   escape   into playful

space.

Space Walker Considers a Broadcast

There is no news here.
It's hard to believe looking back
at earth made into art
the memories I have
all those bulletins at breakfast
or with a cold beer before dinner
the constant parade of mayhem
the sheer brutality of
our human project steeped in gore
to sate our everlasting hunger
the greed, rapine, conquest.
I carry it with me. Escape is

temporary. What after all is this
journey across blank space?
All explorers know the death wish
testing extremes to make
meaning from an encounter with
the existential void, turn negative
to positive. Maybe. Or die in the
attempt, affirming irony.
Here, alone, I embody it all.
I own the voracious appetite,
the bloody mind, ambition and
the deranged quest for lasting fame.

Here, I am the news.

Space-Walker's Escape and Encounter

            Up here
there's no sex
            treading the inky night alone
a cool freedom
ices   the monastic mission
            of the suburban spaceman:

            to see
the world whole
with no one staring
back
            to puzzle
how can this
perfect O
be accident?
            In this
reality show
            being becomes   lightly
bearable

not weighed down by taxes
mortgage, super, the demands of
the week-end car-wash
trimming suburban lawns
in the rotten damp where fear
masquerades as rectitude
and love speaks the language
of cash-exchange

            imagine
re-charging
            the batteries beyond

gravity

        cultivating a space

                to call your own

beyond powerful illusions

illusions of power:

see how small that man
at the lectern looks
soaping soft, slippery words
to fox and box you in.

If only
I could send
back   a bulletin
        of how–it–is

                out here

intimations   of meaning
ex nihilo   the whisper
I heard from a tired God

but think   I've lost   the code.

        Earth seems
    suspended   in night
a coloured orb   flashing in the cold
    a disco ball   after lights out
      and the dancers have all
        gone home.

Space Walker's Secret Mission

Space walking
                you don't travel far—
It's a paradox.
                To journey all this way
                and then tread weightless   for a while
                should be about discovery
but I'm not sure.

Maybe it's
                a delusion   a distraction
an evasion
                a way to avoid awkward truths.
                Maybe I should be confessional.
                Would that make things more   authentic?
Probably not.

I've heard sermons
                urging truth and honesty.
Impossible I say
                without complete self-knowledge.
                Who has it? Let me be   honest
                tell you the truth
when I set out

I craved attention
                to be noticed
something to do
                with feeling invisible as a child
                but now there's something
                else at stake. While the camera's on
I'm trying to
                transmit diligent images

of a desperate world
        for public consumption but before
        I return to the enclosing capsule—
        both prison and haven

the best moments
        are off camera
attempting some fun
        with a private project
        I've embarked upon:
        learning to dance without   gravity

in mystery black
        going nowhere fast
                illuminated
only   by starlight.

Space Walker Out of his Depth

It can be moody
    encapsulated
between moon and earthlight
    the existential angst
of astronauts intrudes:
    how little we are
how   big   the   planetary sky
how quick our time

how long   the aeons   of the   universe.

    Tempted to praise
what should reason worship
    or find sacred but itself?
Is it possible to speak of faith
    without sounding credulous?
What image might suffice
    to hold the mystery?

Dogma won't do.
    Religion needs to
              bend
       and warp

like the space-time continuum

    learn to play with sub-atomic
particles.

    Sure, God isn't Super-Daddy
with a white beard, but maybe
    the unspeakable

beyond the weirdness
      of scientific metaphor:
accelerating gravity

          burrowing black holes

      in the fabric   *of reality.*

Does this help allay the terror
      of our smallness or our violence
our carelessness towards the poor
      and the planet I orbit
without progression

      addicted to this

           privileged space?

Space Walker Hears from Mission Control

Light
      stepping
           through the void
performing a
        liberty jive
              to your own
rock-god soundtrack
        it's possible
            to delude yourself
for a few moments
        exhilaration.

                But really there's no escape
                from the mother ship and big daddy
                plotting from mission control; they will
                soon bring you back to responsibility,
                the tether binding to the morbid past,
                the fearful future, even if you pretend
                for a moment to ignore the intrusive airways,
                cut out the interference make their voices
                dead to you, they haunt your steps
                insisting on sobriety, application,
                fidelity to their shibboleths,
                after all who's funding the project,
money doesn't grow on trees etc.
Think of your career,
I hear them preach,
(everyone is careering).
Don't forget profit
explore something useful
be inspirational,
it's the least you could do:
we need our heroes.

Space Walker Overhears Gossip
from Mission Control

He's
really
down
 to
earth
they say
really good
terms of endearment
for an admired colleague
which leaves me wondering
what that makes me
and my desire
to float   around   up here?

It's true I've been known to call a spade
a bloody shovel in my time, but only
because barrowing soil never seemed exciting.
What does it mean to be grounded?
Feet firmly planted. Not given
to flights of wild fancy or strict imagination,
no particle physics then or metaphysics
more stolid, rooted in loam, perhaps,
but not, you understand, a hippy, that would be
to go too far altogether, suggest airiness,
water, flow, the Age of Aquarius, and such,
no good at all.
                    I'm thinking of my beloved,
gardening—what comfort she finds in the
struggle for fruit and flower and vegetable—
the wrestle to tame nature's profligate
growth—the weeds, the weeds are everywhere.

As we create
so must we destroy.
                    head-in-air
even Johnny-
the falling, f
ailing
astronaut
must
come
down
from delusions of
immortality
and consider
broad maxims
concerning the futility
of flight, the ubiquity
of dust and ashes,
our communion
with the process of soil,
the digestion of worms.

Space Walker Forgets to Dance

Sometimes there is   only bewilderment
flailing in the night   while the days hurtle
you know the direction but can't see the map
not sure who   or what is in control
but it seems   power is not your thing
some other weird impulse   compels you
to shoot for the moon   yet you know
              the final destination
is six feet under or   scattered on earth but
the way isn't plain.   The further forward the
journey goes   losses proliferate   deepen
questions with no answers   multiply:
what reason teaches   reason will not suffice
is acknowledgement
of mystery   wisdom?
Are we all on mission   impossible
trying to fathom   the abyss
making marks on   a blank page
as if we might read   the stars as they wink and twinkle
their mocking eyes   keeping their secrets
while somebody   somewhere croons
a lullaby about   a space cadet
who lost   his mind?

Space Walker's Nightmare

inside

          It's when the spaces bloom

you know you're lost.
No escape from perpetual

orbit

          obsessive loops of thought
patterns that fall into

vacancy

          the recurring struggle to
penetrate the mysteries

of mind

          fill emptiness through invention.
Memories surface like fragments of

a dream

          inviting some willing puzzler
to stitch the pieces   create

a narrative

          which might suffice for a time
before suspicions of self-

delusion

          unravel the tapestry
wipe the board back to black

leaving you

          lost astronaut   questing for some reliable
light to shine the way to inside

out.

Space Walker Confesses

I have chosen   this solo flight
self-isolation   encapsulated
soaring away   from   fire   flood and plague
the frothing rhetoric of   blustering leaders
democracy strangled   by   inequality and greed.
There was a time   I would have been
at the barricades   with a desperate placard
the peaceful demo   the solidarity march
strikes   petitions   protest votes . . .
But nothing happened.   The mayhem got worse.
Now I embrace   loneliness
this useless   exploration
whose value *is*   its uselessness
like crying   in the wilderness

                    not for sale.

Space Walker's Playground

                                        gravity
                          without

           the fun
                    and
    tumble
                                    of
        one

                        last

  solo

                    twist

      a spaced   out
                    acrobat

                            clown

              forward

                        rolling

        in dizzy
                    delight

      would be
                    a serious joke

    without

                            gravity

Space Walker's Epiphany

Sometimes space is less

        blank page

and more blackboard

emphasising the fragility

        of inscription

the easy erasure of chalk

like writing on sand and

        waiting for the tide

the dustbin of history beckons.

        Are all explorers navigating their own

emptiness

        hoping to reach the place of fulfilment:

        the top of the mountain   the elusive pole

an inland sea

        or Eldorado stuffed with gold?

        Shooting for the moon is no different

survival

might mean a moment of success

cash in the bank   a reputation maybe

a gong or two

but does it confer significance

or deepen the mystery of space?

What if the exploration

discovers the stars as so many

chalk marks

against the infinity of endless night

treading darkness

nothing

on a screen will save you.

It is only learning

how to dance on earth alone

in a vacant room

that
will suffice.

Space Walker Considers Re-Entry

It's mental up here   mental as anything:

        this   the only place of escape

the space you make for yourself

        an illusion at least of freedom

though it's hard to shuck off

        the increasing

            weight of years

the growing loss

the hopelessness of politics.

But somehow out of infinite night

        these plates of light

the beckoning stars

        appear calling us back

to belonging:

        we are all made from the same dust

all bodies shattered

        and heavenly at last.

Here   simultaneously   you can see

        the long and short perspective

the shallow streams or

        infinite depths

            of mind

        reaching to grasp the expanding

universe.

        I persuade myself this is where

I want to be:

on mission impossible

trying to realise something new—

one small step etcetera.

And for inspiration I remember

my three-year-old grand-daughter

staring up on a cold clear night saying

Moon. Oh Wow! Her eyes round

with delight

flying saucers reminding me

how love sends me exploring

and love brings me

down

      to earth

            once more.

III

VIEWS FROM THE MUNDANE—

Inferno,
Purgatorio,
Paradiso.

Views from the Mundane Inferno

I'm led by the ghost of a grieving poet
through lost places, places of the lost
in north and southern hemispheres
discovering the baleful cost of decadence.
I walk across ruined ground where demolition
has left scarred acres of broken stone and weeds
leading to dank railway arches where the homeless,
bearded and unkempt, congregate with cheap cans,
drinking until they scream and fight and sprawl.
By the deserted bus-interchange I stumble over
a dead rat soaking in a puddle and hurry on
into town where high street shops are boarded up,
their piss-stained doorways house rough sleepers
with their rags and bags and dogs. Drug-thinned youths
slouch past sucking desperate cigarettes, heads down
and hooded like acolytes of some perverse order,
they are denizens of lost estates condemned from birth
to a toxic inheritance of crime and unemployment:
this is the suicide capital of the land.
There's never enough wealth for salvation,
though the steps of those blessed with cash,
lead from the graffiti-strewn streets
of used needles and broken dreams
to the only place of worship: the glittering Mall.
Here everything is for sale and nothing sacred,
masked people wander through tiers of desire
in an everlasting search to fill the void.
The light is artificial, the air re-circulated.
Outside for days on end, the sky is filled
with orange smoke—the forests are burning,
farmland flooded or dried to a cracked map;
birds fall dead from the air, the sea is poisoned,

vengeful viruses breed, multiply, mutate;
all this screened on a loop of news
along with stabbings, shootings, rape and theft,
the hopeless lines of refugees who long to join
those who scour the stores for redemption.
In the distance through the smog I'm led
to stone white palaces of greed where
the rich and powerful chant the words of a
dying creed, the shibboleth of growth, at any price:
they would feed sugar to the chronically obese;
even the best of politicians, ground under the heel
of ruthless ascension, are corrupted by the eternal
wrangle for power and position. Who can promise
riches loudest and longest and send the people
uneducated, half educated, stuffed with lies,
back to the temple of possession,
reality screened by fake news, adverts,
the trivial clamour of social media?
Banks of lawyers stand by to defend the wrong:
the scales of justice rarely show correct weight.
Further east, also isolated in ivory,
another tower block shows through smog,
like a broken lighthouse on a distant promontory,
where intellectuals are locked in closed circles
of endless argument, deconstructing themselves
 in everlasting theories, playing the game
of scholarly citation, they snake and ladder,
discussing the shades of narcissi, leaving
the juggernaut of global capital and finance
rolling on towards authoritarian tyranny.
History is forgotten, selective relativity
the fashion; every story a power-grab;
truth auctioned to the highest bidder.
Scientists fiddle with mysterious particles,
artificial intelligence, the rule of the algorithm
no brave new world. How to live is not their business.

All this I saw is what we've made. No escape.
Love a memory of what might have been,
the abandoned paradise, the common wealth,
the rational dream to which there seems no way back.
Amid the wreckage I stood and feared,
the human project failed.

The Latest Bulletin

Since the forest fires across the bay
the sea is full of ash, burnt leaves, debris.
There is no news today.

A hooligan bug spreads a plague
depression smoulders through charcoal towns
since the forest fires across the bay

our hungry leaders bluster and bray
the creed of greed geared to power.
There is no news today.

Celebrities preen in idle display
living the decadent dream gone wrong
since the forest fires across the bay.

The unsolved murder, the drunken affray
the abused children, the priest accused:
there is no news today.

The spur is profit, the currency pain.
None of this is news. Be entertained.
Since the forest fires across the bay
there is no news today.

In the Wilderness

Hauling timber on Mount Agony Road,
For our sins, the labourers say, with a grin
spitting on their hands, the bullock-dray stuck
in the mire, the forest dense on either side.
This won't save you, another laughs, *best to think
of rum and tucker* on the other side.
The old hand says nothing, feeling the weight
on the chains like the dead-wood of the past,
the lopped burden of memories he drags.
He thinks of disappointed parents abandoned
in a distant land, the pose he adopted
of the roaring boy in nights of dissipation,
his faithlessness to young women when,
blinded by desire, he jilted them in tears,
knowing to wed them would be a lie;
the sister who died as he held her hand—
his failings as a father of a disabled son,
the limits of compassion over-reached;
all the words unspoken or mis-spoken,
the loose speech of the ungoverned tongue.
Not believing, he confesses to himself,
but cannot know forgiveness. There is only
this struggle and dreams of building over the hill.
Some have visions of a new community
where justice and equality breed peace.
When he was young this was his passion.
Now, he only longs for the descent
to the white crescent of the perfect bay,
the home beside the sea, the lovely
woman who waits for him, cultivating
her abundant garden to feed them well.
That's all he wants or asks. But first this struggle
on the steep road by which most of us must go,
for who could ever be good enough?

In Salford. Friday, April 18th, 1930

The man in the armchair before the open fire,
his book, cigarette and glass of whisky to hand,
is snug in the curtained parlour with its aspidistra
glooming against uncertain light which shimmers
on the polished walnut casing of the wireless.
He has been listening to a broadcast of *Parsifal*.
Before that was a poetry reading—the words didn't
linger in his mind; he prefers crime like the
Agatha Christie on his knee to which his eyes return
when not distracted by Wagner's lush concoction—
the story of a Holy Fool seeking the grail against
the sexual grain. Idly, he thinks he might prefer the sex.
There's an intermission for the bulletin at eight forty-five.
He braces himself for the catalogue of mayhem and misery.
Instead, an announcement in that clipped, cut-glass accent
of the upper-class: *There is no news tonight.*
Piano music follows. He doesn't know whether to be pleased
or disappointed. After all, no news is good news,
don't they say? But he's uneasily aware of missing
the litany of violence and disorder, of foreign machination
and political disaster, the chaos which makes him so *thankful*
for his modest job, his modest wage, his modest pleasure.
He makes a cup of tea. Ready for *Parsifal,* Act III.
While the kettle boils, he considers what it might be like
to live in the old days before there was *news*. Perhaps people
were happier then. Would it, for instance, have been preferable
not to have heard about the doings at Golgotha?
He imagines the newsreader announcing the execution
of a mis-guided revolutionary with two other felons,
the poor weather and the modest crowd of onlookers?
Maybe an interview or quote from the grieving mother.
It comes to mind because it's Good Friday. That's why,

he realises, there is no news and why the opera
featuring the grail knight is about to start again.
He sits back down, lights another cigarette.
The piano music ends, an aria begins.
There's no knowing what to make of Wagner.
It's rich and thick and sickly with strange significance:
like molasses it might be medicinal and maybe
even more sado-masochistic than the news.
He turns to *The Murder of Roger Ackroyd.*
At least there will be an answer to the mysteries there.

Beata

In late summer sunshine, I walk up from the beach,
wave at Belinda, my barber, then the barrista boys
at Café Crumb. I go on past the Pizza joint on the corner,
its notice in the window: *Apologies we will be closed
Friday to Monday. Our son Andrew is getting married.*
Up Crag Road to the junction with Ocean Street,
turn left into Wattle Crescent and along to our place.
Home, I walk up the stairs into the open-plan light,
look out to sea, the sandy crescent I've just strolled,
there's maybe a sail in sight or motor boat scoring bubbles
across the blue towards the wooded farther shore,
the uneven line of the purple mountain backdrop.
Is that some weather coming in, I say.
Not forecast for a while yet, you reply.
Then we sit on the deck in the warmth,
above the flourishing garden you've made
with its berries, fruit trees, vegetables;
its roses for remembrance, flowers for joy.
And if six o'clock should come by, I'll say,
Champagne or Chardonnay? Or maybe I'll have a beer.
We'll sit and sip our drinks, and one of us
will say how blessed are we? Chinking glasses,
we know some who would scoff: *sentimental*
or *too simple* or some other argument
for strangulation of all delight; we'll smile
for a moment, try to forget the venal world
and banish the fear this loving place,
our little piece of Paradise,
depends on someone else's hell.

IV
THE DANCING MAN

Walking on Walbunja Country

His morning walk along the deserted beach
by glittering waters where river meets ocean,
the light incomparable, clean and clear etching
striations of the island's rock as if it is

the work of some fine artificer's pen,
the top-knots of wind-bent eucalypts
are fringed against the blue. It is the place of
dolphin, sea-eagle, stingray, bream.

Daily he walks and imagines,
ghostly, the colonial cutter, Snapper,
Lieutenant Robert Johnston in command,
anchored out there, 30th November 1821,

who named the island for his vessel—
his crew transported to this alien paradise,
pressed and oppressed from the back street
hovels of Portsmouth, London, Liverpool,

barefoot tars nimble in the rigging,
living for rum and to avoid the lash.
In evening hours they raise their voices
to a seasoned fiddle sawing a shanty

and cast their eyes inland to see
beyond the coastal fringe of shrubs and trees
they don't yet know to name acacia, eucalypt,
the smoke of fires rising from the forest.

The next day they sailed into the bay
and up the river Johnston named the 'Clyde',

it being a discovery, he said, despite the several fires
on the banks of people who when approached

showed no symptoms of hostility but *entered freely*
into conversation through interpreters.
These were and are the Walbunja people of the Yuin nation,
traditional owners and custodians of the land,

the beach, on which our walker finds himself between
history and the present, between the early colonists
of the Snapper and the old people of the Walbunja,
their fires, their culture, their dreaming stories,

which he respects but knows he can neither belong to
nor fully understand, just as he fails the test of faith
in bible, cross and capital which underwrites colonial
ambition and still persists in whited sepulchres.

He can't walk backwards to make things right,
though every day there's sorry to say
for the griefs of dispossession,
the mayhem of colonial violence and oppression.

But maybe like his ancestors, the backstreet sailors
with their fiddle, dance and homesick shanties,
he can raise a little music to reach out in hope,
with roles reversed, to learn Indigenous wisdom

concerning preservation of this peerless land,
and find in praise of Dolphin, Sea Eagle, Stingray, Bream,
in mountains, forest, beach, and ocean
some common ground for spirits' meeting place.

The Dancing Man I

(A homage to Zachary Richard)

After duelling harmonicas,
when the band kicks in,
the blues man has all the moves
to his own tune.

There's a shiver, a shimmy,
a little hip swivel,
there are tap steps, two steps,
a liquid sway,
there's a knees-up stomp,
a shoulder shake,
he sings danse danse en Français.

There's concertina knees,
a soft shoe shuffle,
an angled stamp,
swivel and turn,
a hop, a jump,
a sly gyrate,
he sings danse, danse the Zydeco way.

Tired of solo he skips across the stage,
invites the backing singer
to the pop ballet.
There's a sugar push,
a rolling pass,
a wraparound,
and a little kiss.
There's a jiggle and a jive,
an audacious swing,
danse, danse the Cajun way.

Words won't sashay,
only the body can
move these freeze frame
frolics and dance ... dance
the blues away.

On the Last Round

(i.m. Peter Porter)

In our last phone conversation,
speaking of dying, you said
It's like playing golf on a different planet,
and you the least likely of golfers.

It was part of the point, of course,
like Twain you viewed the game as
something to spoil a decent walk
preferably to the nearest watering hole;

that, and the sheer unreality of making
progress toward unbecoming; how impossible
to figure sleep without dream or waking:
the unimaginable extinction of being.

You moved on to talk of my poems,
said I should let in more air and light,
so now as I write I imagine your
slow swing of the club to the ball,

the thrill of sweet-spot timing,
a great looping arc towards the green,
the incomparable feeling you described
of words writing themselves

powered by a mysterious force,
dropping into the exact creative place,
your poem's perpetual ending:
a miraculous, marvellous hole in one.

Last Painting: *Waiting at the Styx*

(After Arthur Boyd)

Late afternoon, the man in the blue canoe
rests on his paddle. We imagine
a slow drift. From our vantage
high on the other side, the kayak
seems to merge with the river;
our explorer could be half-
submerged, but he is so still
we know this cannot be.

Above him, the white rock rears;
cubist angles accentuate
slender pencil lines—eucalypts
striving towards the sun-stained blue.
Heat presses, but on the water may be
a cooling breeze. At the base of the cliffs
a dark arch beckons, tempting passage
to the cave of all or nothing answers.

But the man in the blue canoe
is relaxed, unperturbed. He wears
an old felt hat, jaunty cone
redolent of holiday, ringed
with tiny flowers, stars of earth,
feather-crested, nature's casual
detritus: the colour of flight.
Nothing moves. He sits and breathes.

This is said to be his last painting—
drunk, he confided to a friend
the saddest thing: 'Art is just
another racket.' And then, as if
to prove there was something more,

he undertook this final journey,
brush-stroking towards a restful pause,
before the tide, himself the ferryman.

To a Poet, Going Blind

(For Syd Harrex.)

I heard news you'd joined the seers,
blind in your cabin, looking to the hills,
where still the muses visit, your amanuenses,
who are writing large those mazy figures,
which chart the staggering progress
of the drunken boat with its heavy cargo
of loss and longing through waves of grief.
Your onward surge suggests the darkness
is not implacable; light shines inside out
by which we all might navigate:
the stars are braille to guide a blind man's eye:
I see your fingers reach for them and read.

Charlotte's Grace

(For my grand-daughter)

Coming in with stones from the garden,
your first impulse is to make them shine.
Washing rocks, you call it, and give them
full treatment, soap and flannel and rinse,
your three-year-old hands and eyes intent,
absorbed. This is not a one-off game;
it becomes a favourite. As if
to establish your own ritual,
you show the pebble to me gleaming,
in your eyes and palm the offer of a gift.
I finger the treasure smooth and damp
and see how even grey might offer a gloss
on elemental wonder and variety;
though it dries back, the sheen gone,
stone and water and gift abide,
suggesting through silent invention
sermon and parable: child's play.

Tantrums

(for my grand-daughter, Olivia)

The sudden tempest summons me,
howling in with no warning,
a perfect storm of incoherent
screams, tears and stamping.
I recognise this rage
against the inability
to dredge words which might
explain a cruel predicament:
the way the world with its
obstinate people won't bend
to your will. And as I hold
your small shuddering frame
whispering calm and quiet,
I think of my own long years
of kicking against the way of things,
my anger for an idea of perfection,
and wish you to an easier
and quicker knowledge:
how we cannot mould the world
to heart's desire,
though sometimes we must try;
love steps lightly free
of power and control:
acceptance does not mean defeat.

The Dancing Man II

Neither the frenzied drug-fuelled ecstasy
of the mosh-pit nor the arcane politeness of ballroom
(all those bow ties, frills and furbelows)—
no tights or outrageous leaping across the expensive stage
throwing a slender ballerina to the Gods—
imagine instead a more private joy—
late at night warmed by slow whisky,
a man listening to ballads,
electric in waltz time,
he begins to move to a keening soprano,
bass, guitar, and drums, through the ground floor
of the vacant house without formality
but with the slow step, light skip and twirl
of some old folk footing preserved in his bones.
And as he dances, he thinks of all he has come through:
the tethers of his upbringing, the gilded cage
of career, the disappointments and failure,
the death of son, sister, parents, friends,
chasms of loss. Yet here he is
for a moment elated,
the dancing man, liberating
the embodied poem
he always dreamt he might be.

Intimations

If only we had another word for you, not God,
the Mighty Force, the Great Creator,
beyond metaphysical sludge or busy argument,
not father or mother, the old oedipal snare,
but always beyond the easy judgement or
automatic sneer, like the clarity of sea or stream
on a sparkling day, stone, shell and fish
bright limned beside the bathing feet
or the fine-drawn striations of granite,
the toll-gate islands in glassy light
and beyond the bay the clear and curving line
of the mountains at dusk or dawn.
There is also the simplicity of visitation:
a king-parrot in his crimson and green cloak
edging closer to my granddaughter's feeding hand.
If only we could see beyond such mystery,
marry signifier with signified,
beyond the cosmic dust of broken stars
from which we are all made,
discover you, the first and final
unspeakable word.

Faith

This   is my

poem   place

of worship   of praise

dedication   homage

to a sacred   space

for spirit   without

religion   and with

contemplation   a prayer

devoted to the processes

of life and death, generation and re-generation, the wonder and the love first felt

in the old Saxon Church at Overton above Froda's Ham on the hill that thin place

of ancient settlement where the whisper of the old faiths can be heard shivering

through stone and tree and fern.   In the dim and purple light I sang

in the choir and stared in awe   at the girl with the golden hair

her soaring voice and afterwards   on our bracken bed kissed her and

mouthed the canticle of desire the   craving of flesh for the touch of grace

this is

the path

down to

earth

Pageantry

A still spring morning on the beach,
for the first time in days, no breeze,
the water in the bay flat calm, I was
thinking as I walked of the millions
of tiny shells that crunched beneath
my feet, the filigree intricacy
of their design, such delicate
homes: how much abundant life
is hidden from us. I allowed my gaze
to rise and look out to sea,
the ragged line of the mountains
misty against the blue. It was then
I saw them, five black swans
in effortless cruise, single-file flotilla,
their slow elegance a demonstration
of all we are not, a contrast to
flagged warships or vain parades
with blaring brass and banging drum,
displays of power which suggest
how insecure we feel our place here,
how needy the quest to make certain
our uncertain home. The swans
continued serene in their element.
One lifted a great wing. I saw the flash
of white feathers on the underside,
a shock of surprise. It was as if
for a moment I saw both creature
and angel and knew I was a stranger
to their habitations, yet recognised
in the certain glide, the hidden paddle,
something of majesty, an inhuman
guide to wild revelation.

Out of the Box

My grandmother taught me
when I was young
how two disjunct squares
joined by parallel lines
made a cube or cage.
I've doodled this space
in so many margins
of my life and added
a matchstick figure
behind prison bars
trapped by strict geometry.

But now my art is shifting.
The stick man reaches
and pulls at the ledge, heaving
beyond the self
inscribed thin pencil walls,
escaping bars of inheritance
towards strange intimations—
the possibility of liberation
from the confines of straight lines
to a becoming
again in numinous space—
the blank and waiting page.

Afterword

The poems in this collection respond to the death of my parents (my father in 2018 and my mother in 2020) as well as attempting to navigate the social and political turmoil of our times. The Space Walker sequence, which has had a long gestation, explores in more distanced and metaphorical terms issues raised in the autobiographical reflections. Here, and in some of the other poems, I've enjoyed playing with the 'space' of the page—a return to experiments I tried and abandoned some thirty years ago.

In the face of fire, flood, plague, environmental catastrophe and political chaos the challenge is, in Auden's words, to 'Show an affirming flame'. Accordingly, these poems attempt to move from grief and loss towards consolations, however limited these might be. Intimations of connection and inter-dependence between all living things is the fragile basis for a first step towards spiritual re-orientation and an art of hope.

Notes

'Totem IV': 'Mother Goose' (or Mère l'oye) has a long and complex history from the seventeenth century in France and Britain as the imaginary narrator of tales and nursery rhymes. She later became a character in pantomime.

'Days of Coincidence': Llanddwyn Island is a small island off the west coast of the larger island of Anglesey in North Wales. In Welsh 'Llanddwyn' means Church of St Dwynwen. As the poem makes clear, she is the Welsh patron saint of lovers.

'Museum Pieces III': The phrase 'Goody Two-Shoes' derives from a children's story *Little Goody Two Shoes,* which was first published in England in 1765 and continued to be popular throughout the Victorian era. The plot concerns an orphan girl, Margery Meanwell, who is so poor she has only one shoe. When a benefactor gives her a pair of shoes, she tells everyone she has two shoes. Later, Margery becomes a teacher and marries a rich widower. Her virtue has been rewarded and her wealth well earned. The use of 'Goody Two-Shoes' to denote someone who is ostentatiously virtuous or well-behaved seems to be an implicit critique of the simple morality of the original story.

'The Three of Us I': 'Season of mists and mellow fruitfulness' is, of course, the opening line of Keats's 'To Autumn'. The third stanza of the same poem begins with the question, 'Where are the songs of Spring? Ay, where are they?'

'Space Walker Out of his Depth': I allude here to a phrase used by Amanda Gefner in a BBC production . . . 'space-time can become so warped that it turns in on itself, burrowing a hole in the very fabric of reality'. www.bbc.com/Earth/story/2015 More recently I encountered the same phrase used by Anna Zellen in an article about Black holes on Prezi.com. I'm uncertain as to the original provenance of the phrase.

'Space Walker Considers Re-Entry': As many readers will be aware, 'Mental as Anything' is the name of an Australian pop-rock band. The name of the band derives from the phrase 'mental as anything', late 1970s slang for 'being crazy, outlandish, having extreme fun or "going off"' (Wikipedia). Space Walker enjoys the multiple resonances of the phrase.

'View from the Mundane' section: Recent Work Press published the international anthologies *No News* eds. Paul Munden, Alvin Pang, and Shane Strange in 2020 and *Divining Dante* eds. Paul Munden and Nessa O'Mahony in 2021. The following poems were written in response to these projects, although a third 'No

News' poem was preferred for the anthology and only 'Beata' was included in the print anthology, *Divining Dante*. The Inferno and Purgatorio poems appeared in the electronic edition.

'Last Painting': *Waiting at the Styx*: I'm indebted to Darleen Bungay's biography, Arthur Boyd: A Life (Allen and Unwin, 2007) where I discovered Boyd's remark about art as 'a racket' and his painting, *Waiting at the Styx*.

'Dancing Man I': The poem was inspired by Zachary Richard's performance of his song 'Johnny Danser' which can be found on YouTube under the title 'Danse, Danse'. My poem makes no claims to accurately describe his wonderful dance moves!

'Walking on Walbunja Country': The words in italics are taken from a letter of Robert Johnston to F. Goulburn, the Colonial Secretary, dated 10th December, 1821, regarding his exploration and naming of the Clyde River. The letter is reproduced in *Clyde River Chronicles,* Vol. I 1770–1900, ed. Dianne Hantas.

Acknowledgements

I would like to thank the editors of the following print and on-line magazines in which a number of these poems previously appeared: *Australian Book Review* (States of Poetry, series 1, 2016.); *Axon: Creative Explorations; Meanjin; Meniscus; Transnational Literature.* Other poems appeared in the following Recent Work Press anthologies: *No News,* eds. Paul Munden, Alvin Pang, Shane Strange; *Divining Dante,* eds. Paul Munden, Nessa O'Mahony; and, *The Book of Birds,* eds. Penelope Layland and Lesley Lebkowicz. My grateful thanks to the editors for including my work. An early version of the first 'Space Walker' poem appeared in *Take Five 08* (Shoestring Press, UK). I'm immensely grateful to John Lucas for inviting me to be the contributing editor of that collection, and for his ongoing support of my work. Thanks also go to Peter Monaghan at ArtSound Fm for broadcasting several poems and to Kimberly K. Williams for including sound recordings of poems on the website she curated for the Poetry on the Move Festival in 2021 and 2022. I'm delighted that my poem 'Beata' was chosen for the Poetry Jukebox Project arising from the *Divining Dante* anthology. The Jukebox was situated at the Italian Cultural Institute in Dublin from March to May 2023. My thanks to Nessa O'Mahoney and Maria McManus for their curatorship of this project.

Thanks to Andrew Sant and Lesley Lebkowicz, who offered perceptive comments about individual poems included here. Thanks also to Andrew for introducing me to the wonderful music of Zachary Richard. I benefited from several conversations with Kimberly K. Williams about the experimental use of space in poetry and was encouraged in this direction by some of her recent work. Penelope Layland provided her incisive editorial expertise, which resulted in various improvements to individual poems and the book as a whole. Shane Strange continues to be the ideal poetry publisher. His generosity and selfless devotion to this pursuit are nothing short of heroic. I also benefited from his advice as to the arrangement of poems within the collection.

'It is a true error to marry with poets/ or to be by them'—so wrote John Berryman. My love and gratitude as ever go to Claire for both marrying me and being by me all these years. As well as being the first reader and re-reader of these poems, Claire also lived them with me. No words are enough . . .

About the Author

Adrian Caesar was born near Manchester in the UK but has lived and worked in Australia for over forty years. He was formerly Associate Professor of English at UNSW@ADFA and subsequently taught Creative Writing on an occasional basis at ANU. He is the author of twelve books including non-fiction, fiction, and poetry. His experimental non-fiction novel, *The White* won the Victorian Premier's award for non-fiction and the ACT Book of the Year in 2000. His novel, *The Blessing,* was long-listed for the Voss Literary Award in 2016. His poems have also been long and short-listed for various awards including the Judith Wright Prize, the Dorothy Porter Prize, The University of Canberra International Poetry Prize.